"... I have touched the four corners of the horizon, for from hard searching it seems to me that tears and laughter, love and hate, make up the sum of life."

—ZORA NEALE HURSTON

ZORA NEALE HURSTON:
AFRICAN-AMERICAN WRITER

BY DEBORAH CANNARELLA

The Child's World

Published in the United States of America by The Child's World®
PO Box 326
Chanhassen, MN 55317-0326
800-599-READ
www.childsworld.com

An Editorial Directions book
The Child's World®: Mary Berendes, Publishing Director
Editorial Directions, Inc.: E. Russell Primm, Emily Dolbear, Lucia Raatma
and Sarah E. De Capua, Editors; Linda S. Koutris, Photo Selector; Alice Flanagan,
Photo Research; Red Line Editorial, Fact Research; Tim Griffin/IndexServ, Indexer;
Melissa McDaniel, Proofreader

Cover photograph: Portrait of Zora Neale Hurston/ © Corbis

Interior photographs ©: Beinecke Rare Book & Manuscript Library, Yale University Library: 15, 23, 28, 29, 33,
34; Corbis: 2, 14, 25; Bettmann/Corbis: 6, 9, 13, 16, 18, 20, 24, 27 left; Historical Picture Archive/Corbis: 8;
E.O. Hoppé/Corbis: 19; Marion Post Wolcott/Corbis: 31; Pictorial Parade/Getty Images: 21; Vivian
Hurz/Getty Images: 30; Frank Driggs/Hulton Archive/Getty Images: 27 right; Frank Capri/Hulton
Archive/Getty Images: 35; Library of Congress: 32, 36; Collection of the Maitland Art Center, CM 72.2.8: 11;
Schomburg Center for Research in Black Culture, Prints & Photographs Division, The New York Public
Library: 22; Sheen Educational Foundation Library and the Rare Book & Literary Manuscript Collection,
University of Florida Library, Gainesville: 17.

Library of Congress Cataloging-in-Publication Data

Cannarella, Deborah.
Zora Neale Hurston : African-American writer / by Deborah Cannarella.
p. cm. — (Journey to freedom)
Includes index.
Summary: Profiles Zora Neale Hurston, whose childhood love of stories led her to a successful
career as a folklorist and author of poems, novels, short stories, and plays.
ISBN 1-56766-649-3 (Library Bound : alk. paper)
1. Hurston, Zora Neale—Juvenile literature. 2. Novelists, American—20th century—Biography—Juvenile
literature. 3. Folklorists—United States—Biography—Juvenile literature. 4. African-American novelists—
Biography—Juvenile literature. 5. African-American women—Biography—Juvenile literature.
[1. Hurston, Zora Neale. 2. Authors, American. 3. African-Americans—Biography. 4. Women—Biography.]
I. Title. II. Series.
PS3515.U789 Z645 2002
813'.52—dc21
2002002861

Contents

THE CHARACTERS FROM THE *BRER RABBIT* STORIES BY UNCLE REMUS. ZORA NEALE HURSTON LISTENED TO THESE AND OTHER STORIES ON JOE CLARK'S PORCH WHILE GROWING UP IN EATONVILLE, FLORIDA.

The Center of the World

Zora Neale Hurston loved stories. She loved to listen to them and she loved to tell them, too. When she was young, she would hide in the bushes and listen to the men on the front porch of Joe Clarke's store. The men told **tall tales** and **folktales**—funny stories and stories that taught a lesson. Each man took a turn trying to tell a story that was even better than the one before. They called their stories "lies."

Zora soon learned about Brer Rabbit and Brer Fox and other animals that could talk and act like people. She heard stories that had been told over and over again by **African-Americans** in her town and in other places, too. For the rest of her life, Zora remembered the "lies" she heard on Joe Clarke's porch.

Zora also loved to read. When she was in fifth grade, two white women visited the classroom. When they heard Zora read aloud, they were so impressed they gave her candies and pennies. Later, they sent her a box of books and clothes. "The books gave me more pleasure than the clothes," Zora said. She loved the stories of Hercules and the talking snakes in *The Jungle Book,* written by Rudyard Kipling. She read the adventure stories of Robert Louis Stevenson, the fairy tales of the Grimm Brothers, and the Greek and Scandinavian **myths** and **legends.**

Soon Zora began to make up stories of her own. She made up stories about talking birds and trees and about men who turned into alligators. She also made up stories about the objects in the world around her. In one of her stories, Miss Corn-Shuck falls in love with Mr. Sweet Smell, a bar of the fragrant soap her mother saved for guests.

AN ILLUSTRATION FROM *THE JUNGLE BOOK* BY RUDYARD KIPLING.
AS A CHILD, ZORA LOVED READING THIS BOOK AND MANY OTHERS,
INCLUDING FAIRY TALES, LEGENDS, AND ADVENTURE STORIES.

Zora often sat high in the chinaberry trees that grew beside her front gate. She liked to imagine what the ends of the world were like. She would look out at the horizon all around her. It made her feel as if she were at the "center of the world." She would ride to faraway places in her mind on her imaginary horse.

Other times, she sat on the gate and waved to the travelers in their cars and carriages. She asked them to give her a ride, and sometimes they did. She would ride with them a short distance down the road and then walk back home. When her parents found out what she was doing, she was punished. But Zora had a strong desire to travel and see the world. Her mother said that someone must have sprinkled "travel dust" around the doorstep when Zora was born.

ALABAMA WAS MADE MOSTLY OF SMALL TOWNS AND WOODS WHEN ZORA WAS BORN THERE IN 1891. WHEN SHE WAS STILL QUITE YOUNG, HER FAMILY MOVED TO EATONVILLE, FLORIDA.

Zora was born on January 7, 1891, in Notasulga, Alabama. Her father was John Hurston and her mother was Lucy Ann Potts. John Hurston was a sharecropper. Sharecroppers are farmers that work on other people's land for money. John was also a Baptist minister and he had taught himself to read and write. He wanted to find a better job and make a better life for his family, so they moved to Eatonville, Florida.

Eatonville was the first African-American town that was also run by black people. Zora had many brothers and one sister—Hezekiah Robert ("Bob"), John III, Richard, Joel, Sarah, Benjamin Franklin, and Edward Everett. John Hurston was elected mayor of Eatonville three times and even wrote some of the town's laws.

Zora had a happy childhood. The family lived in a large house on lots of land. The yard was full of oranges, grapefruits, tangerines, and guavas. In the summer, mockingbirds sang all night in the trees. Alligators swam in the lake, and Zora had to chase them away to swim there herself. In the evenings, children from town played hide-and-seek and other games in the Hurstons' big barn and grassy fields.

After supper every night, Lucy helped her children with their homework. "How I hated the multiplication tables," Zora wrote later, "especially the sevens!" When the lessons became more difficult, Lucy could no longer teach the children. Bob, the eldest, took over the lessons, and Lucy stayed to listen. Zora learned to read before she went to school.

When Zora was thirteen years old, her happy childhood ended. Her mother had been visiting a sister who was ill. When she returned, Lucy herself became ill and soon died. Zora was very close to her mother. They were alike in many ways. "That hour began my wanderings," Zora wrote. "Not so much in geography, but in time. Then not so much in time as in spirit."

Lucy always encouraged her daughter's bold spirit. She told all her children to reach for their dreams, to "jump at de sun." For the rest of her life, Zora remembered and lived by her mother's words.

A PAINTING BY JULES SMITH OF EATONVILLE, FLORIDA, WHERE ZORA WAS RAISED. THIS WAS THE FIRST AFRICAN-AMERICAN TOWN THAT WAS RUN BY BLACK PEOPLE.

Wanderings

Two weeks after her mother died, her father sent Zora to a **boarding school** in Jacksonville, Florida. For the first time, Zora saw how black people outside Eatonville were treated. She learned about the **Jim Crow laws** that kept blacks and whites apart. Whites and African-Americans—or "coloreds" as they were called—had separate drinking fountains. Blacks and whites went to separate schools and rode in separate cars on trains.

At that time, some white people feared black people, and some even hated them. Many African-Americans were ashamed of their ways of talking and doing things. They tried as hard as they could not to be noticed. Some did not even dare look a white person in the eye. Zora was shocked. In Eatonville, she had learned to be proud of herself, her neighbors, and their way of life. She could not believe that people would not like her because of the color of her skin.

Zora missed Eatonville and "the lakes, the wild violets in the woods and the animals I used to know." Her father did not pay for her food or her room at the boarding school. She earned money by scrubbing stairs and cleaning kitchens. School officials paid to send her home, but her father and her new stepmother did not want Zora to live with them. For five years, Zora moved from house to house, living with friends and family. She was often unable to attend school.

When Zora was nineteen, she got a job as a housekeeper. She didn't like cleaning, however. Instead, she told wonderful stories to the two little girls in the house. The children loved her, but the older maid did not, and soon Zora was fired. She had many different jobs over the years, but she didn't like any of them. Zora finally realized that she wanted to go back to school.

In accordance with Jim Crow laws, blacks and whites had to use separate water fountains. They also used separate seating areas and waiting rooms in public places.

In 1914, Zora's brother Bob invited her to live with him in Memphis, Tennessee. He said he would send her to school, but he could not send her right away. He asked Zora to help his wife around the house for a while. Zora was disappointed, but she loved taking care of Bob's three children—Wilhemina, Winifred, and Edgar—and they loved the stories she told them.

While Zora Neale Hurston was living in Tennessee, one of her friends told her about a job. The lead singer in a traveling musical show was looking for a maid. Hurston's friend bought her a new blue dress and her friend's daughter lent her a hat for the job **interview.** The singer hired Hurston, and when the show left to tour the South in 1915, Hurston went, too.

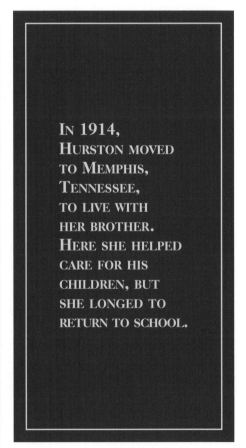

IN 1914,
HURSTON MOVED
TO MEMPHIS,
TENNESSEE,
TO LIVE WITH
HER BROTHER.
HERE SHE HELPED
CARE FOR HIS
CHILDREN, BUT
SHE LONGED TO
RETURN TO SCHOOL.

The group performed a style of music called **light opera.** Hurston loved listening to them, and she learned a lot about music. She also became friends with the cast members. One of the men let Hurston read many of his books.

When the group reached Baltimore, Maryland, the singer gave Hurston a hug and some money and said good-bye. She was getting married and no longer needed a maid. Hurston was alone in a strange city, but she did not lose hope. "Maybe everything would be all right from now on," she thought. "Well, I put on my shoes and I started."

The night school in Baltimore was free, so Hurston signed up for classes. Her English teacher was Dwight O. W. Holmes. Hurston called him a "pilgrim to the horizon." She loved the poems he read in class. He knew that Hurston had talent and he encouraged her, just as her mother had. In 1917, Hurston entered Morgan Academy, part of Morgan College, a school for African-Americans.

ZORA NEALE HURSTON UPON GRADUATION FROM MORGAN ACADEMY. THIS ACADEMY WAS PART OF MORGAN COLLEGE, A SCHOOL FOR AFRICAN-AMERICANS

Hurston got a job helping the wife of a minister named Reverend Baldwin. The Baldwins had a large library, and Hurston memorized many of the poems in their books. She was afraid she would never have the chance to read them again. Hurston liked school, especially her English and history classes. She was so good at making speeches that she won a prize.

Hurston's friend May Miller was a student at Howard University in Washington, D.C. Miller encouraged Hurston to go to Howard, too. Hurston was thrilled but nervous. Howard University was the largest and most famous African-American college in the United States. She knew she would have to work hard to succeed there.

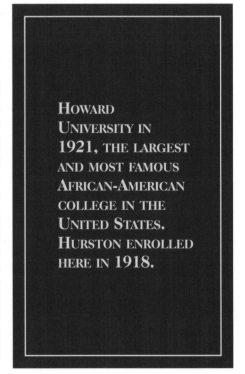

HOWARD UNIVERSITY IN 1921, THE LARGEST AND MOST FAMOUS AFRICAN-AMERICAN COLLEGE IN THE UNITED STATES. HURSTON ENROLLED HERE IN 1918.

In 1918, Hurston moved to Washington, D.C. She worked as a waitress and as a manicurist in a black-owned barbershop for whites. In September, she began classes. As a child, Hurston had talked to the spirits of the trees in Eatonville. Now she told the spirit of Howard University, "You have taken me in. I am a tiny bit of your greatness. I swear to you that I shall never make you ashamed of me."

Hurston got As in the courses she liked and Fs in physical education and the other courses she didn't like. Herbert Sheen was also a student at Howard University. He and Hurston met and fell in love. "For the first time since my mother's death, there was someone who felt really close and warm to me," she wrote. They remained close even after he left to attend medical school in Chicago.

HURSTON WITH FRIENDS AT HOWARD UNIVERSITY. SHE DID WELL IN THE CLASSES SHE LIKED BUT FAILED THOSE SHE DISLIKED.

Hurston's teachers encouraged her to write. One of her stories won a contest in *Stylus*, a literary magazine at the university. The story, "John Redding Goes to Sea," was based on the folktales that Hurston had heard on Joe Clarke's porch. It was published in the magazine with her poem "O Night."

Charles Spurgeon Johnson was the editor of a magazine called *Opportunity: A Journal of Negro Life.* He liked Hurston's story and asked her to write something for his magazine. In 1924, she sent him "Drenched in Light." In this story, a little girl swings on the gate in front of her house in Eatonville, calling to travelers who pass. Hurston used her memories of life in Eatonville in many of the books and stories she wrote.

In January 1925, Hurston went to New York to become a writer. She arrived "with $1.50, no job, no friends, and a lot of hope." In May, she won prizes in a contest held by *Opportunity* magazine for her play *Color Struck* and her story "Spunk." More than 300 people from the **literary** world of New York attended the awards dinner. That dinner changed Hurston's life.

CHARLES SPURGEON JOHNSON, EDITOR OF *OPPORTUNITY: A JOURNAL OF NEGRO LIFE*. JOHNSON WAS IMPRESSED WITH HURSTON'S WRITING, AND HE ASKED HER TO WRITE A STORY FOR HIS MAGAZINE.

NEW YORK CITY IN THE 1920S. WHEN HURSTON ARRIVED HERE, SHE HAD NO JOB AND NO FRIENDS, BUT SHE HOPED TO SUCCEED AS A WRITER.

THE LAFAYETTE THEATER IN HARLEM. THIS SECTION OF NEW YORK CITY WAS AN EXCITING PLACE FOR WRITERS, ARTISTS, AND MUSICIANS DURING THE 1920s, A TIME KNOWN AS THE HARLEM RENAISSANCE.

"Love of Talk and Song"

During the 1920s, black writers and artists from all over America came to New York City. There was a great interest in the writings, art, music, and dance of African-Americans. Harlem, a black section of the city, became the largest African-American neighborhood in the United States. Many white people attended plays, concerts, and readings in Harlem. Some even gave money to black artists to help them get started. That period in history is known as the Harlem Renaissance.

One of the judges of the *Opportunity* contest was Fannie Hurst, a best-selling white writer. She liked Hurston and hired her as a live-in secretary. Soon, the **novelist** discovered that Hurston could not type very well. So Fannie Hurst hired Hurston to drive her around New York and keep her company instead.

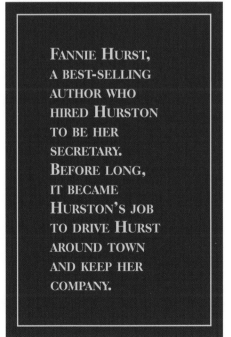

FANNIE HURST, A BEST-SELLING AUTHOR WHO HIRED HURSTON TO BE HER SECRETARY. BEFORE LONG, IT BECAME HURSTON'S JOB TO DRIVE HURST AROUND TOWN AND KEEP HER COMPANY.

Hurston also met Annie Nathan Meyer at the awards dinner. Meyer had helped found Barnard College, the women's college of Columbia University in New York. She helped Hurston get a full scholarship to attend the college. When Hurston began classes in 1925, she was the only African-American student at Barnard.

Hurston was popular at school and also in the neighborhood. Many writers, artists, and musicians met in her Harlem apartment. She became friends with Langston Hughes, Countee Cullen, and other important young writers of the Harlem Renaissance. Hurston was a wonderful storyteller. "She could make you laugh one minute and cry the next," wrote Langston Hughes. She always loved being the center of attention.

COUNTEE CULLEN, AN IMPORTANT YOUNG WRITER OF THE HARLEM RENAISSANCE. HE BECAME FRIENDS WITH HURSTON AND OTHER WRITERS DURING THEIR TIME IN NEW YORK.

In the summer of 1926, Hurston and five of her friends—including Hughes—started a magazine called *Fire!!* They wanted to give African-American writers a chance to express their "fire"—their true feelings and ideas. Most copies of the first issue were destroyed by a real fire. The group could not repay the money they owed and never printed another issue.

In September, Hurston published the first part of *The Eatonville Anthology.* These stories retold the jokes and tall tales that she had heard on the front porch of Joe Clarke's store. They were the kind of stories Hurston loved to tell her friends at her parties in Harlem.

In her first year at Barnard, Hurston discovered a science called anthropology. Anthropology is the study of human beings and their **cultures.** One of her teachers, Dr. Franz Boas, encouraged Hurston to study folklore. Folklore includes the stories, customs, beliefs, dances, and music that people share and pass down to their children.

LANGSTON HUGHES WAS A WELL-KNOWN LITERARY VOICE DURING THE HARLEM RENAISSANCE AND LATER. HE AND HURSTON WERE FRIENDS FOR A TIME.

Hurston loved this new subject. She worked closely with Dr. Boas, whom she called "Papa Franz." She began to think about the "lying" sessions on Joe Clarke's front porch in a new way. They were a part of her childhood, but now she saw that they had a special importance. They were part of the folklore of Eatonville and the black people of the South.

In February 1927, Hurston boarded a train to Florida. She was going to "collect," or gather, folklore in the small country towns of Florida. Her first stop was Eatonville. Hurston borrowed money to buy an old car. She named the car "Sassy Susie."

DR. FRANZ BOAS, ONE OF HURSTON'S TEACHERS AT BARNARD COLLEGE. HE INTRODUCED HER TO THE FIELD OF ANTHROPOLOGY.

When Hurston arrived in Eatonville, the people on the porch of Joe Clarke's store had the "same love of talk and song" she remembered. But Hurston was no longer a young girl eager to hear stories. She was a student from a big university in New York and she acted like one. Her words and actions kept Hurston apart from the people she wanted to talk to, instead of bringing her closer. She did not collect many stories. "Oh, I got a few little items," she wrote, but "not enough to make a flea a waltzing jacket"—which certainly isn't many at all.

ZORA NEALE HURSTON WHILE ON HER 1927 TRIP TO EATONVILLE. SHE AND HERBERT SHEEN WERE MARRIED THAT SAME YEAR.

Hurston met up with her friend Herbert Sheen in St. Augustine, Florida. They were married on May 19, 1927. Hurston wanted to keep working, but her new husband did not approve. They soon decided they could not stay together. Herbert returned to medical school. They could not afford a divorce until four years later, but they remained close friends for many more.

After Herbert left, Hurston went to Mobile, Alabama, to interview a man named Kossola-O-Lo-Loo-Ay, or Cudjo Lewis. He was the last survivor of the last ship that brought African slaves to the United States. Lewis was eighty years old. Nobody knows why, but Hurston copied parts of someone else's article about him and turned in the work as her own. No one discovered what Hurston had done until many years later.

Hurston also visited her brothers Bob and Ben in Memphis, Tennessee. Then she met her friend Langston Hughes. He had never been to the South before. On the way back to New York, they stopped in Tuskegee, Alabama, to visit the grave of Booker T. Washington. They also stopped in Macon, Georgia, to hear Bessie Smith, the famous **blues** singer. The two writers drove Sassy Susie north along the back roads of the South, collecting folklore along the way.

While traveling through the South, Hurston and Langston Hughes visited the grave of Booker T. Washington (left), founder of Tuskegee Institute. They also got a chance to hear Bessie Smith (right) sing the blues.

Genius of the South

As soon as Hurston met Charlotte Mason, she felt they had a strange, strong bond. Hurston believed that she had once met Charlotte Mason in a dream. She even believed that they could read each other's minds from thousands of miles away.

Mrs. Mason was a rich white woman. She gave money to many black artists and writers, including Hurston's friends Langston Hughes and Alain Locke, the editor of *The New Negro* a collection of poetry. Mason wanted to pay Hurston to collect African-American folklore for her. She asked Hurston to call her "Godmother."

CHARLOTTE MASON OFFERED FINANCIAL SUPPORT AND ENCOURAGEMENT TO A NUMBER OF WRITERS. HURSTON WAS ESPECIALLY CLOSE TO HER AND CALLED HER "GODMOTHER."

In 1928, Hurston became the first African-American woman to graduate from Barnard College. After graduation, she traveled to the South to collect folklore for Mrs. Mason. Godmother promised to pay Hurston $200 a month, but Hurston could not tell anyone else what she found on her trip.

During her travels, Hurston visited a lumber camp in Polk County, Florida. The men there had many folk stories and sayings. They sang songs and swung their axes to the rhythm. This time, Hurston tried to fit in, but the people did not trust her. Luckily, she made friends with Big Sweet. Big Sweet made people tell Hurston their best stories. She also set up "lying" contests, which she judged herself.

ALAIN LOCKE ALSO HAD A RELATIONSHIP WITH CHARLOTTE MASON. HE WAS AN IMPORTANT EDITOR AND EDUCATOR WHO URGED AFRICAN-AMERICAN WRITERS TO DO THEIR BEST WORK.

One of the men in camp had a girlfriend who was jealous of Hurston. One night, she attacked Hurston with a knife. Big Sweet told Hurston to run for her life. "When the sun came up," Hurston wrote, "I was a hundred miles up the road, headed for New Orleans."

In New Orleans, Louisiana, Hurston learned about hoodoo. Hoodoo is a type of magic based on African beliefs. She studied with a hoodoo expert to learn the secret practices. Hurston later wrote about hoodoo in her book *Mules and Men,* which was published in 1935.

NEW ORLEANS, LOUISIANA, WAS AN INTERESTING PLACE FOR HURSTON. THERE SHE LEARNED ABOUT HOODOO, A TYPE OF MAGIC BASED ON AFRICAN BELIEFS.

When Hurston returned from New Orleans, she and Langston Hughes began writing a play called *Mule Bone*. It was based on one of Hurston's folktales and had music and dance, too. The writers began to argue about who should get credit for the writing. They never produced the play, and their long friendship ended.

Hurston wrote another show called *The Great Day*. It was about a typical day in a Florida railway camp and included work songs, a sermon, and a "juke joint"—a black music club. Later, Hurston changed the show's name to *From Sun to Sun*. When she performed it for steelworkers in Chicago, she called it *Singing Steel*.

A TYPICAL JUKE JOINT. AT CLUBS LIKE THIS ONE, AFRICAN-AMERICANS PLAYED MUSIC, DANCED, AND ENJOYED EACH OTHER'S COMPANY.

The show was a success, but it did not earn much money. Hurston had stopped working for Charlotte Mason and now she needed money. She published "The Gilded Six-Bits" in *Story* magazine. A book publisher named Bertram Lippincott liked the story and asked Hurston if she was writing a novel. Hurston told him that she surely was—and then she started writing one. One month later, she finished *Jonah's Gourd Vine,* a novel based on her parents' lives.

Hurston was trying on shoes in a store when she opened the publisher's telegram. Lippincott wanted her book! The company offered to pay her $200 right away. Hurston ran all the way to the telegraph office—wearing one old shoe and one new one—to accept the offer.

Lippincott also published *Mules and Men,* the first book of African-American folklore ever written by an African-American. It contains seventy folktales, such as "How the Cat Got Nine Lives" and "How the Snake Got Poison." It also includes songs, music, children's games, and several chapters on hoodoo.

HURSTON PERFORMING AS A HOODOO DANCER. SHE USED THE IDEAS OF HOODOO IN A NUMBER OF HER WRITINGS.

Many African-Americans did not like Hurston's books. They thought black writers should write about the problems black people faced. Hurston wanted to write about how black people lived and how they felt. She said that, even with their problems, African-Americans "go on living and laughing and striving like everybody else."

Mules and Men was published during the **Great Depression**. In five years, Hurston made only $500 from the book. She was poor all her life. She never made enough money from writing to support herself. She always had to take other jobs.

In 1936, Hurston went to Jamaica and Haiti to study West Indian magic. In Jamaica, she saw a medicine man quiet all the frogs in the jungle with just the power of his will. Hurston later published a book about her experiences with folk magic called *Tell My Horse*.

In Haiti, Hurston wrote *Their Eyes Were Watching God* in only seven weeks. This story is about Janie, a woman who falls in love with a younger man named Tea Cake. Hurston had once fallen in love with a younger man she called A. W. P. She loved him very much, but could not give up her work. Hurston's novel is based on her own experience and feelings. Today, it is one of her best-known books.

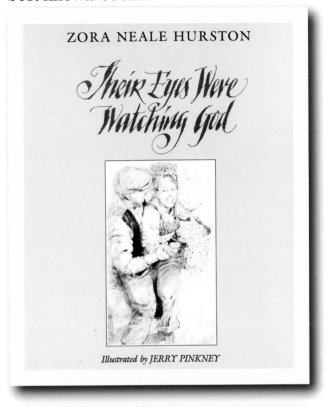

Illustrated by JERRY PINKNEY

THEIR EYES WERE WATCHING GOD, ONE OF HURSTON'S BEST-KNOWN WORKS. SHE WROTE THIS BOOK IN JUST SEVEN WEEKS.

A few years later, Hurston fell in love again. In 1938, she met Albert Price III, a playground worker in Jacksonville. They were married on June 27, 1939. The marriage lasted only four years, and Hurston never married again.

By then, Hurston had published more work than any other African-American woman. People wanted to know more about her, so Lippincott asked her to write the story of her life. In 1942, she published her autobiography, *Dust Tracks on a Road*.

The young wanderer who had left Eatonville continued to wander for the rest of her life. She left New York in 1949 and never returned. She lived on a houseboat, in a trailer, and in rented houses in Florida. She always needed money. She worked as a librarian, as a substitute teacher, and even as a maid. Once, Hurston was cleaning a house while its owner was reading Hurston's article in the *Saturday Evening Post*.

HURSTON IN THE 1930s. BY THE NEXT DECADE, SHE HAD PUBLISHED MORE WORK THAN ANY OTHER AFRICAN-AMERICAN WOMAN.

For a while, Hurston lived in a one-room cabin in Eau Gallie, Florida. She had a little yard and a dog named Spot. She said she was "happier than I have been for at least ten years." She also had flower and vegetable gardens, like those that grew around her childhood home in Eatonville.

In 1959, Hurston became ill. She had to move into the St. Lucie County welfare home. When she died on January 28, 1960, all her books were out of print. Several had never even been published.

A friend collected money to bury Hurston in a cemetery for African-Americans. In 1973, the writer Alice Walker traveled to Fort Pierce to find the unmarked grave. She placed a headstone there to honor the forgotten writer.

ZORA NEALE HURSTON
"A GENIUS OF THE SOUTH"
1901–1960
NOVELIST, FOLKLORIST,
ANTHROPOLOGIST

WRITER ALICE WALKER PLACED A HEADSTONE AT ZORA NEALE HURSTON'S GRAVE. SHE MADE GREAT STRIDES IN REINTRODUCING HURSTON'S WRITING TO THE WORLD.

Zora Neale Hurston believed that African-American people should be proud of their culture. Hurston spent her life collecting and sharing their words, their stories, and their songs. She listened to their many different voices, and she celebrated each one.

Timeline

1891 Zora Neale Hurston is born in Notasulga, Alabama, on January 7. For a long time, people thought Zora was born in 1901 because she often changed her year of birth.

1904 Zora's mother, Lucy Ann Potts Hurston, dies on September 18. Zora is sent to a boarding school in Jacksonville, Florida.

1915 Zora Neale Hurston joins a traveling Gilbert and Sullivan show as the lead singer's maid.

1917 Hurston attends night school in Baltimore, Maryland, and then enrolls in Morgan Academy.

1918 Hurston moves to Washington, D.C., in the summer. She begins classes at Howard University in September.

1921 *Stylus* magazine publishes Hurston 's story "John Redding Goes to Sea" and her poem "O Night."

1924 *Opportunity* magazine publishes the story "Drenched in Light."

1925 Hurston moves to New York. Her play *Color Struck* and her short story "Spunk" win prizes in a writing contest held by *Opportunity* magazine. She begins classes at Barnard College and meets Dr. Franz Boas.

1926 Hurston and five friends start a literary magazine called *Fire!!* Hurston publishes part of *The Eatonville Anthology* in the *Messenger* magazine.

1927 Hurston travels to Florida on her first folklore-collecting trip and marries Herbert Sheen in St. Augustine. She meets Charlotte Mason when she returns to New York.

1928 Hurston becomes the first African-American to graduate from Barnard College.

1930 Hurston works with Langston Hughes on the play *Mule Bone*.

1932 Hurston 's show *The Great Day* is presented in New York on January 10.

1933 *Story* magazine publishes "The Gilded Six-Bits." Bertram Lippincott agrees to publish her first novel, *Jonah's Gourd Vine*.

1935 Lippincott publishes *Mules and Men,* the first book of African-American folklore written by an African-American.

1936 Hurston travels to Jamaica and Haiti to study West Indian magic. She writes her novel *Their Eyes Were Watching God* in just seven weeks.

1937 *Their Eyes Were Watching God* is published in September.

1938 *Tell My Horse* is published in October.

1939 Hurston marries Albert Price III in Florida. *Moses, Man of the Mountains* is published in November. The story is based on the Bible story about Moses, who led his people out of slavery.

1941 Hurston moves to Los Angeles, California, where she works as a story consultant for Paramount Pictures movie studio. She works on her autobiography.

1942 Hurston publishes her autobiography, *Dust Tracks on a Road.*

1947 Hurston travels to Honduras to collect folklore.

1948 Hurston 's seventh and last book, *Seraph on the Suwanee,* is published in October.

1951 Hurston rents the cabin in Eau Gallie, Florida, where she wrote *Mules and Men.* Her beautiful gardens attract tourists.

1959 Hurston suffers a stroke and is forced to move into the St. Lucie County welfare home for care.

1960 Hurston dies on January 28 and is buried on February 7 in an unmarked grave in a black cemetery in Fort Pierce.

1973 The African-American writer Alice Walker visits Zora's grave and places a headstone there honoring her as "A Genius of the South."

Glossary

African-American (AF-ri-kehn uh-MER-ih-kehn)
An African-American is a black American whose ancestors came from Africa.

blues (BLOOZ)
The blues is a type of slow, sad jazz music created by African-Americans.

boarding school (BORD-ing SKOOL)
A boarding school is a school in which the students live during the school year.

culture (KUHL-chur)
A culture consists of the customs, traditions, and way of life of a group of people.

folktales (FOK-tails)
Folktales are spoken stories passed down through generations by word of mouth.

Great Depression (GRAYT di-PRESH-uhn)
The Great Depression was a period in U.S. history when many people were poor and were out of work. The Great Depression began in October 1929 and lasted until World War II (1939–1945).

interview (INT-uhr-vyoo)
An interview is a meeting between someone who is applying for a job and someone who is hiring a worker.

Jim Crow laws (JIM KRO LAWZ)
Jim Crow laws are laws that discriminate against African-Americans.

legends (LEJ-uhnds)
Legends are stories that may or may not be true about events and people of the past.

light opera (LIYT AHP-uh-ruh)
A light opera is an amusing play set to music.

literary (LIT-uh-rehr-ee)
Literary describes people or things related to books.

myths (MITHS)
Myths are stories told to explain natural or mysterious events.

novelist (NAHV-uh-list)
A novelist is a storyteller who writes books called novels.

tall tales (TAWL TAYLZ)
Tall tales are stories that are hard to believe.

Index

FOR FURTHER READING

Books

Calvert, Roz. *Zora Neale Hurston*. New York: Chelsea House, 1993.

Lyons, Mary E. *Sorrow's Kitchen: The Life and Folklore of Zora Neale Hurston*. New York: Aladdin, 1993.

McKissack, Pat and Fredrick, *Zora Neale Hurston: Writer and Storyteller*. Springfield, N.J.: Enslow, 2002.

Porter, A. P. *Jump at De Sun: The Story of Zora Neale Hurston*. Minneapolis: First Avenue Editions, 1992.

Web Sites

Visit our homepage for lots of links about Zora Neale Hurston: *http://www.childsworld.com/links.html*

Note to Parents, Teachers, and Librarians:
We routinely verify our Web links to make sure they're safe, active sites—so encourage your readers to check them out!

ABOUT THE AUTHOR

Deborah Cannarella is an author and editor of history and biography books for children. She has also written several books and magazine articles for adults. She lives in Roxbury, Connecticut.